Sa
the Great

The Herald of Divine Love

Saint Gertrude, pouring out her
compassionate love to Jesus Crucified.

Saint Gertrude the Great

The Herald of Divine Love

"That in all things God may be glorified."
—*Holy Rule of St. Benedict*

TAN Books
Charlotte, North Carolina

Nihil Obstat: ✠ Stephanus Schappler, O.S.B.
Abbas Coadjutor Im. Conceptionis

Imprimatur: ✠ Carolus Hubertus Le Blond
Episcopus Sancti Josephi

Previously published by the Benedictine Convent of Perpetual Adoration, Clyde, Missouri.

Retypeset and republished in 2002 by TAN Books.

ISBN 978-0-89555-026-2

Printed and bound in India

TAN Books
Charlotte, North Carolina
www.TANBooks.com
2014

Contents

St. Gertrude the Great

A Wonderful Saint

ST. Gertrude is one of the greatest and most wonderful saints in the Church of God. Holy Church has distinguished her from all others of her sex by adding to her name the honorable title, "the Great." **Saint Gertrude is the diadem, the queen-flower of the Benedictine Order, the most beautiful lily among the holy virgins who flourished during the glorious middle ages**. For hundreds and thousands of pious Christians, St. Gertrude has become a guide in the spiritual life, a teacher of the most intimate spirit of prayer and familiar intercourse with God. Who can enumerate the hosts of elect souls that have obtained union with God through the pious reading and consideration of her writings? Countless numbers of the blessed jubilantly praise and extol this privileged, favored virgin in whom Our Lord takes His special delight.

1

St. Gertrude was the herald of devotion to the Sacred Heart of Jesus—that sacred cult which has become so dear and which has proved a fountain of consolation and graces to millions of Christians. Our Divine Savior repeatedly disclosed to her His Divine Heart, the furnace of love, as though for her sake He could not await the time decreed by His eternal wisdom for the revelations of his Heart. Devotion to the Sacred Heart was the special characteristic of St. Gertrude's piety. The mystery of mercy and love contained in that Divine Heart had been revealed to her by the Son of God Himself four centuries before it became an object of special devotion to the Church at large. St. Mechtilde, a contemporary of St. Gertrude, and also a Benedictine, shared with St. Gertrude this glorious privilege. Thus the Heart of Jesus had long been an object of adoration and love to the sons and daughters of St. Benedict when, in the 17th century, it pleased God to procure for It, through St. Margaret Mary, that more solemn worship with which It is now surrounded.

One thing is particularly remarkable in the life of St. Gertrude, the like of which cannot be found in the life of any other saint: it is the extraordinary promises made to her by our Savior in favor of those who venerate her.

Testimonies of Gertrude's Sublime Sanctity

Even during St. Gertrude's lifetime, Our Lord revealed her sublime sanctity to many holy souls. Once He addressed these words to a person bound to the saint by the bonds of a holy friendship:

"She for whom thou prayest is **My dove who has no guile in her**, for she rejects from her heart, as gall, all the guile and bitterness of sin.

"She is **My chosen lily which I love to bear in My hands**, for it is **My delight and My pleasure to repose in the purity and innocence of this chaste soul**.

"She is **My rose whose fragrance is full of sweetness**, because of her **patience in every adversity** and the **thanksgiving which she continually offers Me**, which ascend before Me as sweetest perfume.

"She is that **spring flower** which never fades; and I take pleasure in gazing upon her, because she keeps and maintains continually in her breast an ardent desire, not only for all virtues, but for the utmost perfection of every virtue.

"She is a **sweet melody which ravishes the ears of the blessed**, and this melody is composed of all the sufferings she endures with so much constancy."

To another person our Divine Savior thus praised the favorite of His Heart: "I have borne her (Gertrude) in My arms from her infancy. I have preserved her in her baptismal purity and innocence, and she, by her own free choice and will, has given herself to Me entirely and forever. As a recompense for the perfection of her desires, **I, in return, have given Myself entirely to her**. So pleasing is this soul to Me that when I am offended by men I often enter her heart to repose, and I make her endure some pain of body or of mind, which I inflict on her for the sins of others. She accepts this suffering with the same thanksgiving, humility and patience as she receives all that comes from Me, and offers it to Me in union with My sufferings. Thereby she appeases My anger and obliges My mercy to pardon, for her sake, an immense number of sinners."

Jesus showed to another soul a precious stone, the beauty of which cannot be described. "This jewel," said Our Lord, "I always wear as a pledge of My affection for My spouse. By its brightness the whole celestial court knows that there is no **creature on earth so dear to Me as Gertrude**, because there is **no one at this present time** amongst mankind who is so closely united to Me by **purity of intention** and **uprightness of will**. There is no soul still bound by the chains of flesh and blood whom I am so disposed to enrich with My graces and favors. There is no soul who refers to My glory alone the gifts received from Me, with such sincerity and fidelity as Gertrude . . . **You can find Me in no place where I delight more, or which is more suitable for Me, than in the Sacrament of the Altar, and after that, in the heart and soul of Gertrude, My beloved**."

Jesus Himself condescended to reveal to St. Mechtilde: "I have united My Heart so closely to Gertrude's soul by the ties of My mercy, that she has become one spirit with Me."

A similar revelation was made about the same time to another saintly person. Our Savior said that Gertrude would become still more perfect and would attain to so intimate a union with God that her eyes would see, and her lips would speak only what God willed, and all her other senses would be equally submissive to Him.

Gertrude in the Sacred Convent-Garden

In the year 1261, Gertrude, then a mere child of five years, entered the cloistered convent of Helfta, in Germany. This convent had been founded but a few years previously. The community was composed of angelic religious, who with unsullied hearts and childlike faith conversed with Jesus in the most intimate love. An old cloister chronicle relates:

"From the foundation of this religious community, its members led an uninterrupted angelic life for almost ninety years. The Lord Jesus was so familiar with persons of this convent that they conversed with Him as with their dearest Lord and Bridegroom, as a friend speaks to a friend. Also the entire heavenly host had a particular joy and exultation in this blessed community of religious."

Yes, the secluded community at Helfta was Our Lord's holy family. Entirely separated and detached from the world, those pious virgins surrendered themselves, soul and body to their Divine Master, whom in holy love and innocence they had chosen as their Spouse from their tenderest years. They knew that He was really and truly present in their little church in the Blessed Sacrament, just as He is in heaven. From this faith sprang their love for the Divine Office. With burning love their hymns of praise resounded day and night.

How those noble virgins loved silence and recollection! The sweet voice of their Beloved attracted them to loving meditations and affectionate intimacy. As industrious bees draw honey from flowers, so those angelic souls flew to the great, beautiful Eucharistic Flower, immersed their whole being into the depths of Its infinite love, and extracted from It the honey of celestial joy. Words failed them to express the sweetness and kindness of their Lord, the inexpressible delights of His Heart! If holy obedience hindered them from visiting their Beloved, the Lord sought them instead. Everywhere the Heavenly Bridegroom found His chosen souls and held tender converse with the loved ones of His Heart. In them was fulfilled our Savior's promise: "If any one love Me . . . My Father will love him, and We will come to him and make Our abode with him" (John 14:23).

In this sacred convent-garden, Gertrude flourished as a resplendent white lily. **"I delight so much in her,"** said Jesus, **"that I have chosen her as My abode. All that others see and love in her is My work;** and whoever loves My work in her, loves Me. I have decreed that she stand alone, without friends or relatives, that none may love her from ties of relationship, but that **I Myself may be the sole cause of her being loved and esteemed."**

The Wonderful and Privileged Life of St. Gertrude

Truly, this little convent-maid, whose birthplace, parentage and ancestry have remained shrouded in obscurity, became, in the bloom of her youth, the loving confidante of the Divine Master. Gertrude had won not only the Heart of God, but the wonderful charms and innocence of her refined disposition soon made her a favorite also among the pious sisterhood.

"She was," states a religious of that community, "wise and prudent of mind, far beyond her age; clever and full of gentle grace. In school she quickly out-stripped her companions. It was marvelous to see how easily she mastered the sciences. Despite Gertrude's cheerful, open disposition, however, she did not care to take part in play. She preferred, if permitted, to withdraw into the dark, silent church, and there, by the glimmer of the perpetual light, to converse with the heavenly Playmate of her pure childish soul. It was thus Gertrude grew from childhood to womanhood, full of loving innocence."

When Gertrude had reached the proper age, she answered the call of heaven which beckoned her to the venerable Order of St. Benedict. **Like the great Patriarch**, she, too, **was to be filled with the spirit of all the just**. Worldly science and heavenly knowledge were freely imparted to her. **The Lord crowned her with the diadem of His richest and most precious graces, but upon her heart He impressed**, as the sacred liturgy so significantly expresses it, **the seal of His Divinity**.

Gertrude had now reached her twenty-fifth year. Her piety and her many eminent qualities of mind and heart combined to make her the ornament and the treasure of the monastery of Helfta. On the 27th of January, 1281, she was favored for the first time with a vision of her ardently-loved Bridegroom. In her own charming words we give the account of this great event of her life: —

"Since the preceding Advent my heart had been filled with an indescribable longing and unrest, whose salutary effects were to give me a disgust for the frivolities and levity of youth. This was the first step of Thy love in preparing my heart for Thyself . . . I was in the dormitory, just at the beautiful hour of evening twilight. According to the rule, I inclined toward an aged Sister in token of respect. Raising my head, whom should I behold but Thyself, O my Beloved, my Redeemer, the most beautiful among the children of men! Thou didst appear as a most charming youth, who in a friendly and pleasant manner didst approach me.

"Standing before me, Thou didst say in accents of indescribable sweetness: 'Thy salvation is at hand! Why art thou consumed by grief?' Then I felt myself transported to the choir and heard these wonderful words: **'I will save thee and deliver thee; fear not.** Thou hast sucked honey amidst thorns, but **return now to Me—I will inebriate thee with the torrent of My celestial delights.'**

"Thou didst open Thy arms invitingly. I endeavored to approach—but, lo! a great hedge of sharp thorny bushes barred the way. Dismayed, I stood there, bewailing my sins and defects. In a moment, Thou, O Lord, didst extend Thy hand to me, and immediately I was beside Thee and reposed on Thy Heart. My gaze fell upon Thy hands and feet, and I saw, good Jesus, those five glorious Wounds with whose Blood Thou didst pay the ransom of the whole world.

"From this moment," adds the saint, "I commenced to taste only Thyself, O my God. With new spiritual joy I began to follow in Thy footsteps, and I found Thy yoke sweet and light."

Though hitherto Gertrude had been very pious and a model of religious observance, after the above mentioned grace she considered the previous time lost, and believed that, as the prodigal son, she had just returned to her God. From this hour she discontinued all secular studies. One book alone became very dear to her, and its contents daily engraved themselves more deeply upon all the powers of her soul:—

it was the Holy Scripture. To meditate thereon was her greatest delight. God taught her heart to penetrate the most hidden sense of the Inspired Books. She possessed a wonderful facility to use texts from the Holy Scripture to comfort and refresh all who came to her, according to each one's need.

How Our Lord loved His chosen bride! He poured abundant graces in ever-increasing fullness into Gertrude's heart. The humble virgin herself declares: "Thou hast so often melted my soul by loving caresses that if I did not know the abyss of Thine overflowing condescension, I should be amazed were I told that even Thy Blessed Mother received such extraordinary marks of tenderness and affection." That which filled and animated her interior could not remain concealed. The warmth and fervor which emanated from her was poured out upon all her associates.

The Perfect Spouse of Christ

It seems Our Lord raised Gertrude in a short time to that degree of perfection where the soul has **no other will, no other thought, no other life, than**

Christ. This was certainly indicated by the mysterious grace of Our Lord's exchanging His Heart for hers. From this union sprang the sublime virtues which distinguish this incomparable virgin. She was remarkable, above all, for an **unlimited abandonment to the Divine will, a love for God's decrees, even the most severe, a perfect peace of heart, boundless desires for the glory of God and the salvation of the world, and that holy, evangelical liberty which is extolled as the noblest inheritance of the true children of St. Benedict**.

Gertrude's heart sought God alone, and found Him everywhere. To please Jesus in all things was the one aim of her life. A saintly person once prayed earnestly that he might know what virtue attracted Our Lord's greatest complacency in His well-beloved spouse, Gertrude. Our Savior deigned to respond: **"Her liberty of spirit**. This priceless gift includes the deepest self-knowledge and love of God, and leads the soul to the heights of perfection. It disposes the heart of Gertrude to receive, at every moment of her life, graces of inestimable value, and prevents her from attaching her heart to anything which could either displease Me or impede My work in her soul."

Jesus was her all—her constant thought day and night. Every movement of her body and soul was offered to God and directed to His glory. **Unceasing union with her Beloved was Gertrude's life**. Yet she did not neglect her exterior occupations. The happy manner in which she combined active labor with interior union was once manifested to Saint Mechtilde.

This saint beheld Jesus seated on an elevated throne in the church. St. Gertrude was actively engaged in exterior occupations, walking to and fro. But her countenance was always steadfastly fixed upon the Lord and she seemed to drink in with burning ardor the graces which flowed to her from His Most Sacred Heart. At the same time she appeared to fulfill her exterior duties with utmost zeal. St. Mechtilde was amazed at this vision.

"Behold," said Our Savior, "such is the life which Gertrude, My beloved, leads before My face. She walks ever in My presence, never losing sight of Me for an instant. She has but one desire: to know the good pleasure of My Heart. As soon as she has ascertained this, she executes My will with care and fidelity. Her whole life is an unbroken chain of praise consecrated to My honor and glory."

The sanctity of Gertrude's soul diffused itself even over her bodily faculties and irradiated her whole being. She seemed to the exterior eye, like one from a higher world. An indefinable charm hallowed her countenance, which at times transformed itself into a mysterious, superhuman beauty.

Gertrude's life became daily more supernatural; at times she received Divine directions and profound illuminations, whose inspiration seemed to carry her spirit into the fathomless depths of the Divinity; again she was transported into heaven to anticipate its delights, to enjoy its beauty. Often, in holy ecstasies, she was vouchsafed the most delightful intercourse, not only with her Heavenly Spouse, but also with the Blessed Virgin, her Mother and protectress.

Gertrude had her favorites among the beatified friends of God, and frequently the saints came to converse with her. A special attraction drew her toward Saint John, the disciple of love, to whom she bore so striking a resemblance. Her spiritual Father, St.

Benedict, was honored by her with the most filial affection, and he, on his part, rewarded her piety with marks of true paternal tenderness. He chose her to reveal to the faithful the promise he had made, to give special aid at the hour of death to all those who, during life, should have rejoiced with him in the graces that attended his blessed death. St. Gregory the Great, St. Augustine and St. Bernard were particularly dear to St. Gertrude. She loved with a love of preference St. Agnes, the tender spouse of the Divine Lamb, the virgin-martyr, St. Catherine of Alexandria, and St. Mary Magdalen.

All the extraordinary graces received from God and the many tokens of love from His saints were no detriment to Gertrude's humility. She, the marvelously beautiful celestial flower in this barren terrestrial garden, was in her own eyes nothing but a "withered blade of grass." The more the bright rays of Divine Light flooded her soul, the meaner and viler did she seem to herself. "O Master," she once exclaimed, as she walked through the field, "Thou dost work no greater miracle than this, that the earth supports me—me, an unworthy sinner!"

"Ah!" whispered the voice of her Beloved

immediately, "with joy should the earth offer to bear thy footsteps, since the whole heavens await with inexpressible impatience the happy hour when thou wilt tread its precincts!"

St. Gertrude's Unlimited Confidence

Blind trust in God's mercy, unlimited confidence in His love, is one of the secrets to obtain sanctity. The Holy Fathers have always taught that the **measure of** our hope and confidence is the measure of the graces which we receive from heaven. They have realized that, through our unreserved confidence, God is most honored and glorified. Nothing will be denied to an unlimited confidence. Our Lord revealed: "It is impossible that anyone should not receive all that he has believed and hoped to obtain. It gives Me real pleasure when men hope great things from Me and I will always grant them more than they expect."

Saint Gertrude understood that **confidence is the key which opens the treasures of the infinite mercy of God**. To her confidence alone she attributed all the gifts she received, and she invited all to place boundless confidence in our Savior in order to receive from Him immeasurable graces. "All that I have received," she affirmed, "I owe to my confidence in the gratuitous bounty of God." Yes, Gertrude knew that Jesus is an infinite Treasure placed by the Eternal Father at the disposition of all, and that it is His supreme delight, as Savior, to distribute His gifts to those who trust in Him. He frequently complained to the beloved of His Heart of man's want of confidence.

To a religious who had long prayed in vain for a particular favor, Jesus revealed how pleased He was with Gertrude's boundless trust in His goodness. "Why dost thou not act like Gertrude, My chosen virgin?" Our Lord inquired of the nun. "She is so firmly established in My Providence that there is nothing which she does not hope for from the plenitude of My grace. Therefore, I will never refuse her anything." Alas! we creatures have too little knowledge of God's kindness, love, and mercy! Our distrust arises because we compare God with ourselves. Oh, that all hearts would realize that **Jesus is all love, all mercy. He has treasures of grace for all, but few come to bear them away by means of**

their confidence.

In all things, Gertrude had recourse to Jesus as a child has to its mother. Nothing, in her eyes, was too trivial to be recommended to Him. On one occasion, having lost a needle in a pile of straw, she besought Him to find it for her. "O dear Jesus," she said, "vainly, indeed, would I search for this needle. It would be lost time. Please get it for me Thyself." Extending one hand, and turning away her head, she immediately found the needle between her fingers. **Again and again, Our Lord encouraged this confidence so dear to Him**.

"O Jesus, what should I add to these prayers to make them yet more efficacious?" Gertrude once asked. Turning to her with a countenance full of sweetness, Our Savior replied, **Confidence alone easily obtains all things!** . . . Once when St. Gertrude was troubled with temptations, she implored the Divine assistance. Our Lord, in His exceeding mercy, spoke thus to her: "Anyone suffering from human temptations, who flees to My protection with firm confidence, belongs to those of whom I can say: 'One is My dove, My chosen one out of thousands, who has pierced My Heart with one glance of her eyes.' **And**

this confidence wounds My Heart so deeply that were I unable to relieve such a soul, it would cause My Heart a sadness which all the joys of heaven could not assuage . . . The confidence that I truly have the power, the wisdom and the goodness to aid a soul faithfully in all her miseries, is the arrow which pierces My Heart, and does such violence to My love that I can never abandon her."

St. Gertrude's Special Graces

Of the many favors bestowed by the Lover of virgins on His spouse, we may single out four of special importance. The first grace, Gertrude never mentions definitely. She always calls it the **great grace**, and when she attempts to speak of it, her heart immediately overflows with praise and gratitude toward the Divine Giver. From a careful study of her life, however, it is easy to surmise that this grace was the **impression of Our Lord's Sacred Wounds upon her heart**. It was through ardent desire and constant prayer that Gertrude received this marvelous grace. During the winter after Our Lord's first visit, she found this very beautiful prayer in honor of His Passion.

"O Lord Jesus Christ, Son of the living God, grant that I may aspire towards Thee with my whole heart, with yearning desire and with thirsting soul, seeking only Thy sweetness and Thy delights, so that my whole mind and all that is within me may ardently sigh to Thee, who art our true Beatitude.

"O most merciful Lord, engrave Thy Wounds upon my heart with Thy most Precious Blood, that I may read in them both Thy grief and Thy love; and that the memory of Thy Wounds may ever remain in my inmost heart, to excite my compassion for Thy sufferings and to increase in me Thy love. Grant also that I may despise all creatures, and that my heart may delight in Thee alone. Amen."

"This prayer," writes Gertrude, "pleased me very much. I memorized it and recited it frequently. One afternoon, during the same winter . . . I suddenly became conscious that Our Lord had deigned to hear me. I felt, O my God, how Thou didst imprint on my heart Thy adorable Wounds, even as they are on Thy Sacred Body. Notwithstanding my exceeding unworthiness, Thy infinite bounty has even to this hour preserved therein the impression."

It is certain that, as a result of this sacred stigmata, Gertrude suffered excruciating pains the remainder of her life. These pains were inexpressibly alleviated, however, by the new relationship she had contracted with her most tenderly loved Jesus, through love and mutual suffering.

Of the **second grace**, frequent mention is made in her book of revelations. This event occurred during Advent, seven years later, while she was in church assisting at Holy Mass. Gertrude thus describes the favor: "After I had received the Sacrament of Life, I saw a **ray of light, like an arrow, dart forth from the Sacred Wound in Thy right Side**, on the Crucifix . . . It advanced toward me and **pierced my heart**. Then Thou didst say to me: 'May the full tide of thy affection rise to Me, so that all thy pleasure, thy hope, thy joy, thy grief, thy fear and every other feeling may be sustained by My love!'"

During the last year of her life, our saint listened to the discourses of a Dominican Father who spoke most impressively on the love of our Heavenly Master. "Love is like an arrow," he said, "whatever we shoot with it, we may call our own!"

Gertrude's heart glowed with vehement love when she heard these words. "Ah!" she exclaimed in the ardor of her love, "who will grant me that I may obtain such an arrow! Immediately I would transpierce Thee, the Only-beloved of my heart, that I might possess Thee eternally!"

Scarcely had she uttered these words when she beheld her celestial Spouse. He carried a golden arrow in His hand, and said: "Thou didst desire to wound Me; but I have a golden arrow with which I will pierce thee so that thy wound may never heal."

The arrow sank deeply into her heart and wounded her soul in three ways: First, **by rendering all earthly pleasures distasteful**, so that nothing in this world would afford her soul enjoyment or consolation. Secondly, **by exciting an ardent desire in her soul to be united to God**, so that she felt she could not breathe or live apart from Him. Thirdly, **by so transfixing her soul as almost to separate it from her body**, and overwhelming her with the torrent of Divine delights.

As the **third** special grace, we may regard the **interchange of hearts between Our Lord and St. Gertrude**.

Writing of this, our saint says: "Thou hast granted me Thy secret friendship, by opening to me the sacred ark of Thy Deified Heart in so many different ways as to be the source of all my happiness. Sometimes as a special mark of our mutual friendship, Thou didst exchange It for mine!" After the ineffable revelation during which Jesus exchanged His Heart for hers, the holy virgin felt her Divine Spouse live and love within her. This interchange of hearts conceals operations of grace beyond our understanding.

The **transforming and deifying visit of the Infant Jesus to Gertrude's heart** may be called the **fourth** special favor of our saint. Her own account of this grace is exquisitely beautiful: "It was the anniversary of the blessed night of Our Lord's Nativity. In spirit, I tried to fulfill the office of servant of the glorious Mother of God when I felt that a tender, new-born Infant was placed in my heart. At the same instant, I beheld my soul entirely transformed. Then I understood the meaning of these sweet words: 'God will be all in all' (1 Cor. 15:28). My soul, which was enriched by the presence of my Beloved, soon knew, by its transports of joy, that it possessed its Spouse. My thirst for Thee was satisfied by these words: 'As I, in My Divinity, am the figure of the substance of My Father, so also shalt thou be the figure of My substance in My Humanity. As the sun communicates to the air its own brightness and light, thus will I deify thy soul, penetrating it with the rays of My Divinity to prepare thee for the closest union with Me.'"

God not only granted inexpressible graces to St. Gertrude herself, but He also **promised great graces to all who, after her death, should venerate her**.

Glorious Promises

Even during her life, Saint Gertrude's prayers were miraculously answered. Through her intercession, many were delivered from long and serious illnesses. Others were admonished in their dreams to disclose their troubles to her, and were delivered from their afflictions. Our Lord once said to her:—

"If anyone, being oppressed by sorrow and grief, humbly and sincerely seeks consolation in thy words, he will not be deceived in his desires; for I, the God abiding in thee, urged by the liberality of My love and goodness, desire through thee to bestow much good on many. Whosoever commends himself with full confidence to thy prayers will obtain life eternal by thy mediation. Just as much as anyone hopes to receive from thee, so much will he surely obtain. Besides this, whatever thou shalt promise anyone in My Name, that I shall certainly grant him."

St. Gertrude received from the Eternal Truth Himself the most consoling promise that whenever anyone devoutly praises and thanks God for the graces bestowed on her, Our Lord will enrich that person with similar virtues and graces. And if this does not come to pass immediately, it will be fulfilled at an opportune time.

Another time Our Lord promised her that no one who had venerated her would depart this life without having first received the grace of making his life pleasing to God, and that, furthermore, he would enjoy the comfort of a special friendship with God.

Once our Divine Savior, opening His lips and inhaling, said to His beloved spouse: **"Just as I have now drawn in My breath, so shall I in truth draw to**

**Myself all who incline toward thee
with love and devotion for My sake**,
and I shall grant them the **grace to make
progress in virtue from day to day.**"

Our Lord promised Gertrude that if anyone should praise and thank Him for the
graces lavished on her, and ask for a favor,
He would, in that love with which He had
pre-elected her from eternity, assuredly
grant the plea, provided it were for the eternal welfare of the suppliant.*

In addition, St. Gertrude received the
promise that if anyone performs a good
work in her honor, in union with that love
in which God descended from heaven and
accomplished the work of our Redemption,
he should obtain as his merit whatever is
performed in honor of the saint. No sinner
who had loved and venerated her should
die suddenly!

St. Gertrude once asked Our Lord for a
sign as a solemn confirmation of these
favors. "Stretch forth thy hand," said Jesus.
She did so. Immediately He opened the ark

---

* It is remarkable, however, that St. Gertrude does
not seem to interest herself greatly in obtaining
mere temporal and earthly favors for her clients.
Her intercession is particularly powerful for needs
of the soul.

of His Deified Heart, and placed her hand in the Wound of His side. Then He said: "Behold, hereby I promise to preserve inviolable the gifts I have bestowed on thee. If, however, according to My wise foresight, I suspend their effects for a time, I hereby bind Myself to recompense thee threefold, by the omnipotence, wisdom and goodness of the Triune God." When Gertrude withdrew her hand, she saw a golden circlet on each finger, and on the signet finger, three. "Seven rings shall be to thee a certain proof that the seven favors I have promised thee for the salvation of the world have been ratified," said Our Lord.

St. Gertrude and the Sacred Heart

The secrets of the Divine Heart of Jesus have been called the "treasure" which is reserved for latter times. But with regard to His spouse it seems our Divine Savior could not await the time decreed by His infinite wisdom for the revelation of His Sacred Heart to the world at large. Often He appeared to St. Gertrude and disclosed to her ravished eyes the mysteries of the Divinely-human love of His Heart. **He**

made her the herald of this grace-abounding devotion which not until four centuries later was given to the world.

At one time this adorable Heart was shown to her as a **treasury** in which all riches are contained; at another time as a **harp** which is played upon by the Holy Spirit, the sweetness of whose tones ravishes the Blessed Trinity and all the heavenly court. Once It was represented to her as a **fountain**, the delicious and plentiful waters of which refresh the souls in purgatory, strengthen and enrich the just on earth, and fill the blessed in heaven with inebriating delights. Again, she beheld It as a **golden thurible**, whence as many different kinds of fragrant incense ascend to the Triune God as there are various races of men upon earth.

It was further revealed that this Heart is an **altar** upon which the sacrifices of the faithful, the homage of the elect, and the worship of the angels are offered, and on which Jesus, the Eternal High Priest, offers Himself in sacrifice.

Once on the feast of St. John, the beloved disciple, St. Gertrude exerted herself during Matins to praise the disciple whom Jesus loved above the rest of His Apostles and lo! our Savior appeared to her, accompanied by this dear saint, whom He gave to her for a special protector. St. John spoke to Gertrude most kindly, instructed her regarding many mysteries and bestowed upon her precious graces. Continuing his heavenly discourses, he said: "Come, come, beloved spouse of my Master, let us repose together on the sweetest bosom of Our Lord, in which all the treasures of beatitude lie hidden!"

St. John stood to the left, and St. Gertrude to the right of Our Savior. As they reposed on the sanctuary of His Heart, and were ravished with inexpressible delights at Its beatings, this dialogue took place between them: "Well-beloved of the Lord, did these harmonious beatings which rejoice my soul also rejoice thine when thou didst repose during the Last Supper on the bosom of the Savior?"

"Yes, I heard them, and my soul was penetrated with their sweetness even to its very center."

"Why, then, hast thou spoken so little in thy Gospel of the loving secrets of the Heart of Jesus?"

"My mission was to write of the Eternal Word . . . but the language of the blissful pulsations of the Sacred Heart is reserved for latter times, that the time-worn world, grown cold in the love of God, may be warmed up by hearing of such mysteries."

On the same feast, four centuries later, in 1673, Our Lord appeared to St. Margaret Mary, showed her His Divine Heart enveloped by flames of love and said: "My Heart is so full of love for men that It can no longer contain the flames of Its burning love. I must discover to men the treasures of My Heart and save them from perdition."

Another time, while Saint Gertrude recited the Divine Office in the church, she had taken great pains to sing the words and notes with devotion. But from human frailty she still made many mistakes. "Ah!" she thought sadly, "what gain will come to me from such exertion to which is attached such great inconstancy?"

Our Lord, who could not endure to see His spouse dejected, presented to her His Divine Heart, saying: "Behold, I manifest to the gaze of thy soul My deified Heart, the harmonious instrument whose sweet tones ravish the Most Adorable Trinity. I give It to thee, and like a faithful, zealous servant, this Heart will be ready, at any moment, to repair thy defects and negligences . . . Make use of It and thy works will charm the eye and ear of the Divinity."

Gertrude wondered and feared because of this amazing goodness of her Lord. She thought it too great a condescension for the adorable Heart to remain continually near her to supply for her defects. But Our Lord consoled and encouraged her by this comparison:—

"If thou hast a beautiful and melodious voice, and takest much pleasure in chanting, wilt thou not feel displeased if another person whose voice is harsh, wishes to sing in thy stead, and insists on doing so? Thus My Divine Heart, understanding human inconstancy, desires with incredible ardor to be continually invited, either by words or signs, to operate and accomplish in thee what thou art unable to accomplish thyself. Its **omnipotence** enables My Heart to act **without trouble**. Its impenetrable wisdom enables It to act in the most **perfect manner**. And Its joyous and loving **charity** makes It **ardently desire to accomplish** this end."

This is doubtless one of the most beautiful and benediction-bringing revelations ever communicated to any saint. St. Gertrude made good use of it, and daily offered all her exercises in union with the Sacred Heart. She did so especially when she felt incapable of thanking God for some grace. Then she would call upon the Sacred Heart of Jesus to render worthy praise and thanksgiving in her stead. She frequently saw how the Heart of Jesus gave worthy thanks to the Blessed Trinity in the name of all mankind.

St. Gertrude likewise drew from the Sacred Heart innumerable graces for others. Once as she begged Our Savior to enrich with special favors all who had been recommended to her prayers, Jesus said to her: "They may draw forth all they need from My Divine Heart."

St. Gertrude and Holy Communion

The "Bread from heaven" was the nourishment of this virginal spouse of Christ. Gertrude knew well who was hidden under this precious Food, for often her purified gaze was permitted to penetrate the veil, and she beheld her Divine Bridegroom in a state of extreme love and mercy inclining toward the children of men. What must have been the burning ardor with which she approached the Banquet of Love! Yet she was fully conscious of her own wretchedness. She realized how poor is man's preparation to receive the Most High who desires to give Himself to us in Holy Communion. "Behold, already the Bridegroom calls thee," she would say to herself, "but how wilt thou go to Him, since thou hast not the adornment of good works?"

But Gertrude did not dwell on such reflections of her unworthiness. Instantly she placed all her hope in God's goodness by saying: "What will it avail me to hesitate? Even if a thousand years were given me, I could nevertheless not prepare myself fittingly. I will therefore go **to meet Him with confidence and humility**, and when my Lord sees me from afar, He will send in advance a garment wherein I may be fittingly clad to be presented to Him."

Animating her heart with such sentiments, she kept the eyes of her soul directed on her vileness. Our Lord, taking pity on her, sent her the **virtues of His Sacred Heart: His innocence, humility, love** and **confidence**. Adorned therewith, she approached Him, and was most lovingly received by the Eternal Son and the Heavenly Father. Often, too, she would ask the holy Mother of God to adorn her heart and lead her to the altar.

In all Gertrude's writings, among the numberless irresistible invitations of the Heart of Jesus urging men to seek Him in the Eucharist, we find but one passage breathing the spirit of severity. It refers to those communicants who permit their tongue to be stained by sins of uncharitableness and criticism. One day after Holy Communion, as St. Gertrude was thinking with what care she should use her tongue, honored and sanctified as it was above all the members of her body by the Body of Christ being laid thereon in Holy Communion, Our Lord instructed her thus:—

"One who does not abstain from vain, idle, or sinful discourses, and who approaches Holy Communion without repentance, is like a person who gathers a heap of stones at the threshold of his door to throw at his guest when he comes to visit him, or beats him cruelly on the head with a rod."

Once Gertrude felt slightly provoked when she noticed a certain religious approach Holy Communion with extreme timidity. Our Lord rebuked her, however, saying, "Dost thou not realize that **I deserve reverence equally as much as love?** But as human frailty is incapable of rendering both, I inspire one with reverence, and to another I give the unction of My love."

Our Savior often instructed St. Gertrude regarding the **advantages of frequent Communion**. He told her that He longs for all the faithful to approach Him. His Heart is open even to the weakest and most imperfect, if their venial sins are more a consequence of human frailty than of a perverse will. He complains if they absent themselves from this Banquet of Love because they do not see the tenderness of His paternal Heart.

Once, when our saint was about to communicate, she asked: "O Lord, what wilt Thou give me?"

"I will give Myself to thee entirely," He replied, "with all the virtues of My Divinity, even as My Virgin-Mother received Me."

"But," inquired St. Gertrude further, "what shall I gain by this more than those persons who received Thee yesterday with me, and who will receive Thee today, since

Thou dost always give Thyself entirely and without reserve?"

Jesus deigned to reply: "It is a time-honored custom that one who has twice held the office of governor excels in honor him who has filled the office but once. Likewise, **they shall be more glorious in heaven who shall have received Me oftener on earth . . .**

"In communicating but once, the Christian receives Me for his salvation, with all My goods—that is, with the united treasures of My Divinity and Humanity; but he does not appropriate the abundance of these treasures except by repeated Communions. At each new Communion, I increase, I multiply the riches which are to constitute his happiness in heaven! . . .

"He who **communicates from habit does not taste the sweetness of the Eucharist**; whilst he who prepares his heart for Its reception by exercises of piety and devotion, **tastes of this sweetness in proportion to his good disposition**. In fine, he who approaches Me with **fear and reverence is less eagerly welcomed** than he **who comes to Me from a motive of pure love**."

On another occasion Our Savior revealed

to St. Gertrude, in these touching words, the love of His Divine heart in the Holy Eucharist: "My delights are to be with the children of men. To satisfy My love I have instituted this Sacrament. I have obliged Myself to remain therein even to the end of the world, and I wish It to be frequently received. Should anyone deter a soul, **not in the state of mortal sin**, from Communion, he would impede the delight of My Heart. I have done My utmost to manifest the tenderness of My Heart in the Blessed Eucharist. When, impelled by the vehemence of My love, I enter a soul by Communion, I fill it with graces, and all the inhabitants of heaven and earth, and all the souls in purgatory experience at the same moment some new effect of My bounty."

Once after St. Gertrude had heard a long and rigorous sermon upon God's holiness and justice and the great fear with which one should approach the Sacraments, Jesus said to her: "It is not My justice, but My goodness and tenderness, which I strive to manifest in the Eucharist. To be convinced of this, consider how I am imprisoned in a small ciborium, and under what lowly appearances I come to men, I, the King of glory! Even thus is My justice imprisoned by My mercy, My gracious mercy, which alone I extend to all in this Sacrament. Dost thou not see that whilst reducing Myself to the tiny proportions of the Host, I really subordinate My Body, thus humiliated, to the body of him who receives Me?"

St. Gertrude and the Passion of Christ

The saints have always united great veneration for Our Lord's Passion to the worship of the Holy Eucharist. No devotion was dearer to St. Gertrude than devotion to the sufferings of our Redeemer. She bore the Sacred Wounds of Our Lord in a mystical manner in her own heart. She understood how to **read in the Wounds of Jesus**, not only the **greatness of His sufferings**, but also the **intensity of His love**. This grace she obtained by ardent prayer, for she says: "By prayer I obtained that favor, namely, to read in Thy Wounds both Thy sufferings and Thy love." Our Lord Himself urged St. Gertrude to the fervent contemplation of His Passion by making known to her that **she should venerate constantly the love of His Sacred Heart on the Cross**.

Once in answer to an inquiry on the part of St. Gertrude, Our Savior replied: "It would be most advantageous for mankind to know and bear constantly in mind, that I, the Son of the Virgin Mary, remain ever in the presence of My Heavenly Father to whom I offer Myself continually for their salvation. Whenever through human frailty they sin in their heart, I present My most pure Heart to the Eternal Father in atonement. Whenever they offend Him by their evil deeds, I show Him My transpierced hands. Thus in what way soever they sin against Him, the wrath of My Eternal Father is appeased by My merits, so that they will obtain a ready pardon if they will only repent of their sins. I therefore desire that My elect, whenever they obtain pardon for their sins, offer Me their gratitude for having given them so easy a means of reconciliation."

Looking at the Crucifix

Gertrude's eyes ever sought her Crucifix, that sorrowful memento of her Savior's love. At night it never left her hands. Not satisfied with this devotion, she consecrated the whole of every Friday to meditation on the Passion. Jesus once said to her: "It is **very agreeable to Me to see thee thus honoring the Crucifix**. It is always an effect of Divine grace when men's eyes meet the Image on the Cross, and never once do they rest upon It, but their **soul is benefitted**. The **oftener** they do this here on earth with **reverence and love**, the **greater** will be their **reward** in heaven."

One day as Gertrude affectionately held her Crucifix and kissed it, Our Lord said: "Every time one kisses the Crucifix, or looks at it with devotion, the eye of God's mercy is fixed upon his soul. He should then listen within himself to these words of tenderness from Me: 'Behold how I, for love of thee, hang on the Cross—naked, despised, My whole Body wounded, all My limbs distended. And still My Heart is enkindled with such glowing love for thee that if it were beneficial for thy salvation and thou couldst not be saved in any other way, I would for thee alone endure all that I suffered for the whole world!'"

Again and again Our Lord made known to Gertrude the complacency with which He regards those who sympathize with His sufferings. "Meditation on My Passion possesses a value in My eyes infinitely surpassing any other. Even a short meditation upon My Passion is of more value than long and multiplied acts of piety which have no direct reference to My sufferings and death . . ."

However, meditation on His sufferings is the most pleasing to Our Lord when we **imitate** the humility and patience He practiced during His Passion. Our Crucified Lord said to Gertrude: "All the testimonies of love, respect, and reverence which are offered to the Image of My Cross will not be perfectly acceptable to Me unless the **example of My Passion is also imitated.**"

Our Lord also promises to accept most favorably the devout veneration of His five Sacred Wounds, with some petition commended to His Divine Heart.

Uniting Our Sufferings with Those of Christ

Our Savior frequently impressed upon St. Gertrude the exceeding value our sufferings acquire when united to those of His life and Passion. "Whoever in his trials and adversities unites himself with My sufferings, and strives to imitate My patience and resignation, will truly repose on My Heart and participate in all the merits of My life."

St. Gertrude suffered during the greater part of her life. Once when she was confined to bed by illness, this consoling revelation was imparted to her: **Bodily and spiritual affliction are the surest sign of Divine predilection**, yea, even a mark of the espousal of the soul with God. Gratitude for suffering is a precious jewel for our heavenly crown.

If anyone imagines he could bear patiently other sufferings than those laid upon him by the Divine will, let him humble himself before God. **Man should always firmly believe that God sends just that trial which is most beneficial for him**.

St. Gertrude and the Blessed Virgin

Probably no saint has understood better than St. Gertrude the power and necessity of Mary's assistance in the sanctification of souls. Gertrude's devotion to the Mother of God was of a most tender nature. Our Lord revealed to her in many sublime

visions, the grandeur and dignity of His
Virgin-Mother. He manifested to Gertrude
in a thousand ways the law He imposed
upon Himself of communicating His riches
to man only through the hands and Heart
of Mary. When Jesus first began to favor
Gertrude with special revelations, He once
said to her: "I give thee My own Mother as
thy protectress. I confide thee to her care."
In an hour of trial, Gertrude, terrified,
called upon Jesus to help her. He replied:
"I have given thee My own most merciful
Mother for thine, and it is through her I
will dispense My graces to thee. Have
recourse to her in all thy necessities and
thou wilt surely find strength and consolation."

Gertrude celebrated Our Lady's festivals
with a joyful heart, and one these days
expected special favors from her beloved
Mother. Mary herself more than once condescended to associate the humble virgin
with her in the joys of her Divine mater-
nity. From Christmas to Candlemas,
Gertrude received so many tokens of love
from the Divine Child and His Blessed
Mother that without supernatural aid her
heart could scarcely have borne the excess
of love and grace.

On the feast of Our Lady's Nativity, September 8th, Gertrude once asked what reward those would receive who celebrated this feast with fervor. Mary answered: "They will **merit a special share in the joys which I possess in heaven**, and in the virtues with which the most glorious Trinity adorns me!"

The feast of the Annunciation, March 25th, was always a day of particular graces for Gertrude. The wonderful **mystery of the Incarnation** was to her a cause of constant, unspeakable joy. Almost daily she meditated upon the ineffable condescension of God toward Mary and the almost infinite dignity of the Mother of God. And Mary returned this love with her fondest affection, and filled Gertrude with heavenly gifts.

Once, on the vigil of the **feast of the glorious Assumption**, August 14th, Saint Gertrude begged Our Lord to obtain for her the favor of His sweet Mother, for she feared she had never been sufficiently devout to the Blessed Virgin. Jesus inclined most graciously toward His Mother and in a fond embrace manifesting the most filial affection, said: "Remember, O Mistress, Mother most loving, that **for thy sake I**

am merciful to sinners, and regard My elect one as if she had served thee all her life with due devotion." Mary then gave herself entirely to Gertrude, for the sake of her Divine Son.

What Is Most Pleasing to Jesus

"What would be most pleasing to Thee at this moment, O Lord?" Gertrude once inquired. "What does Thou desire of me?"

"Place thyself before My Mother, who reigns at My side, and endeavor to praise her." Following this advice, Gertrude greeted the Heavenly Mother as the paradise of delights, the most beautiful habitation of God. She besought Mary to give her a heart so replete with virtues that God would take pleasure in dwelling therein. This good Mother adorned Gertrude with the rose of love, the lily of chastity, the violet of humility, and the heliotrope of obedience.

Once Our lady appeared to her under the form of a spotless lily with three petals. One petal stood erect, the other two drooped. By this Gertrude understood that Mary is justly called a resplendent lily of the Trinity, because she, above all creatures, received most perfectly and most worthily the favors of the Triune God, and never sullied her soul with even a shadow of sin. The upright petal signified the omnipotence of the Father, the two drooping petals, the wisdom of the Son, and the benignity of the Holy Spirit, which qualities each of the three Divine Persons communicated to her in such a degree as to produce in her a vivid resemblance to Himself.

She also learned from the Blessed Virgin that when anyone piously greets her with these words: "O radiant Lily of the ever-peaceful Trinity! O resplendent Rose of heavenly charm!" Mary bestows favors upon him according to her power, through the omnipotence of the Father, the wisdom of the Son, and the benignity of the Holy Spirit. Mary added: "And to him who greets me thus, I will appear at his death in the bloom of such beauty that he shall enjoy a foretaste of heavenly comfort and sweetness." After this revelation, Gertrude often greeted the holy Virgin with these words:—

Hail, fair Lily of the ever-peaceful and glorious Trinity! Hail, effulgent Rose of the heavenly court, of whom the King of heaven willed to be born

and nourished with thy milk! Feed our souls by the effusions of the Divine influences.

St. Gertrude and the Poor Souls

St. Gertrude entertained a deep compassion for the souls in purgatory. At Holy Communion she besought our loving Savior with tender, fervent petitions, to be merciful to these dear sufferers. Once, before Communion, as she reflected with heartfelt pity on the sufferings of the holy souls, it seemed to her that she descended with our Lord into the depths of purgatory. There she heard Jesus say: "At Holy Communion I will permit thee to draw forth all to whom the fragrance of thy prayers penetrates." After Holy Communion Our Lord often delivered more souls than she dared to ask for.

Once Gertrude prayed with particular fervor for the faithful departed. On asking Our Lord how many souls His mercy would deliver, she received this reply: "My love urges Me to release the poor souls. If a beneficent king leaves his guilty friend in prison for justice's sake, he awaits with longing for one of his nobles to plead for the prisoner and to offer something for his release. Then the king joyfully, sets him free. Similarly, I accept with highest pleasure what is offered to Me for the poor souls, for **I long inexpressibly to have near Me those for whom I paid so great a price**. By the prayers of thy loving soul, I am induced to free a prisoner from purgatory as often as thou dost move thy tongue to utter a word of prayer!"

Our Savior also instructed Gertrude for whom she should pray most. On the day when the community commemorated in common the death of their parents, our saint saw the happy souls ascend from dense darkness like sparks from a flaming forge. She inquired if all these were relatives. Our Lord replied: "I am thy nearest relative, thy father and thy mother. Therefore, My special friends are thy nearest relatives, and these are among those whom I have liberated."

"Herald of Divine Love"

God's object in imparting to St. Gertrude so many wonderful revelations **was to manifest His infinite love for man**. "It is the love of My Heart which has inspired thy writings," Jesus said to His spouse when He commanded her to write the revelations she had received. Gertrude, in her humility, hesitated to publish these singular favors, but Our Lord conquered her repugnance by saying: "Be assured, thou wilt not be released from the prison of the flesh until thou hast paid this debt. **I wish these revelations to be, for later ages, the evidence of My love to draw souls to My Heart.**" When our saint asked the Savior what title she should give to her book of revelations, He responded: "This book shall be called **Herald of Divine Love**, for in it the sweetness of My Divine love will in some measure be tasted."

"But," said Gertrude in astonishment, "the persons who are called 'heralds' appear with high esteem. What authority wilt Thou give to this book, since Thou dost deign to give it such a title?"

Jesus answered: "To each one who reads in this book for My honor, with the right faith and humble devotion, with grateful sentiments and a desire of being edified, I grant remission of venial sins, the grace of spiritual consolation, and the ability to receive still greater favors."

Many of St. Gertrude's revelations deal

with the sacred liturgy and the Divine Office. The reading of her works without explanation would therefore not prove as profitable as might be expected to persons unfamiliar with the liturgy.

Glorious Death of St. Gertrude

Saint Gertrude's heart had become a glowing furnace of love for her heavenly Bridegroom. She longed with unspeakable longing for His summons to the heavenly joys. Her life, it is true, had been one of most intimate union with Jesus, because Our Lord had appeared to her with astonishing frequency, nay, almost daily. To quote a pious author, we may say that Gertrude "lived at home with her Beloved." The sight of His beauty in these visions and the caresses of His love had so ravished her soul that she awaited, with holy impatience, the day when He would take her to His Heart and unite her to Himself forever. How often she sighed for death in the words of the psalmist: "As the hart panteth after the fountains of water, so my soul panteth after Thee, O God! My soul hath thirsted after the strong, living God; when shall I come to appear before the face of God?" Yet her ardent desires were unheeded by Jesus; He deferred His coming. But the longer He delayed, the stronger grew her intense desire to be with Christ her Spouse.

As Gertrude once reflected on death, she exclaimed: "O Lover of my soul! I have never honored Thy saints worthily. I am undeserving of their consolation in my last moments. I can expect comfort from Thee alone, the Sanctifier of saints." Jesus consoled her by responding: "At the hour of thy death **I Myself will appear to thee with all the joys and charms of My Divinity and Humanity.**"

Later, when Gertrude's heart seemed almost overcome by the vehemence of its love and the intensity of her desire for death, she exclaimed: "When, oh, when wilt Thou fulfill Thy promise to deliver me from the prison of my body, and permit me to enter the beatitude of eternal life?"

"Do I not," replied Our Lord, "during the time of this delay, give thee, My love? I refer to the tender and intimate union which is accomplished with thee here on earth in the Sacrament of the Altar, which, after this life, can no longer take place in such a manner."

On another occasion when Gertrude lovingly complained of her banishment in this world, Our Lord encouraged her to bear her exile by manifesting to her the manner of her death. She was rapt in ecstasy and beheld hosts of angels and saints, with censers in their hands, coming to meet her. Then followed the patriarchs, the prophets, the apostles, the martyrs, the virgins, even the holy innocents. Evil spirits dared not approach.

At length Gertrude became seriously ill. She was filled with joy when she learned that no hope was entertained for her recovery. She turned to Jesus with these words: "Although **I desire above all things**, to be delivered from the prison of the flesh, and **to be united to Thee**, nevertheless, if it pleased Thee, I would willingly remain on earth and endure the severest **sufferings even until the day of judgment**."

Our Lord replied: "Thy good will so moves My Divine goodness, that I accept it as if thou hadst accomplished what thou desirest."

Gertrude had received from her Divine Bridegroom the promise that **she should die of Divine Love:** that the ardor of her love for Him would truly consume her life. Often Gertrude had swooned away under the overwhelming power of her vehement love, and now its intensity was inflicting upon her that **glorious death**, even death from excess of love! The consolation vouchsafed to her in her last illness were so abundant that they were imparted even to those who attended her. She suffered unspeakable pain for several months before her death, but so great was her fervor that she insisted on being carried daily to assist at the adorable Sacrifice.

After manifold sufferings and almost life-long infirmities, she now neared her death. In indescribable sorrow, her sister-religious surrounded her bed. Jesus appeared to her, His Divine Countenance radiant with joy. At His right hand was his holy Mother, and at His left the beloved disciple, St. John. Our Lord was attended by an immense multitude of angels, virgins and other saints. He approached the bed of the dying saint, showing such marks of tenderness and affection as were more than sufficient to sweeten the bitterness of death.

The Sisters were reading the Passion at Gertrude's bedside. When they pronounced the words: "And bowing His Head He gave up the ghost," Jesus leaned toward His faithful spouse, opened wide His adorable

Heart, and in a transport of love, poured forth all Its tenderness upon her. Celestial spirits surrounded her bed; she beheld them inviting her to paradise, and heard them singing in accents of ravishing melody: "Come, come, come, O mistress! the delights of heaven await thee. Alleluia! Alleluia!"

The happy moment of Gertrude's release had come. A religious heard our Divine Lord address her thus: "Behold **now thou art to be united to Me and to become My own forever**, by the sweet embrace which I will give to thy soul. I will present thee to My Eternal Father by the close embrace of My Heart."

At that instant, Gertrude's holy soul, escaping from its earthly tabernacle, rose toward Jesus and penetrated the sanctuary of His sweetest Heart. Who can picture the welcome and the caresses she received from her Divine Spouse! Who can conceive the joy and thanksgiving of the angels and saints as they attended her triumph! Excess of Divine love had, indeed, consumed her life. The golden arrow foreshown to her by Jesus had wounded her soul; it had pierced her heart through and through, and her angelic spirit had taken flight to the place she had chosen for her repose in life and death—the Heart of Jesus.

As the community prostrated in prayer for the soul of their beloved Gertrude, they beheld her standing before the throne of the Most Holy Trinity, radiant with glory, interceding for those who recommended themselves to her prayers. One religious beheld our Savior invite her to His Heart. There the favored Gertrude shall rest throughout eternity. There, so closely united to her Beloved, she obtains precious gifts for her devoted clients from that inexhaustible Treasury of grace.*

St. Gertrude's Method of Prayer

St. Gertrude's prayers are of heavenly beauty. Only the blessed Spirit of Jesus Christ who dwelt within her heart could have animated her mind with such loving affections and ardent effusions of devotion. In these prayers, her soul expresses, with charming simplicity, what it feels and desires. Instructed by her celestial Spouse, and consumed with love for Him, Gertrude knew how to season her prayers with irre-

---

*In the Benedictine Order the feast of Saint Gertrude is celebrated on November 17th. (✝ 1302)

sistible charm and grace. She understood
perfectly how to unite her prayers with
those of His holy Mother and the saints.
Her prayers thus possessed almost infinite
value and irresistible efficacy before the
Heavenly Father.

The style of prayers of this seraphic
daughter of St. Benedict is most noble and
unique. As an introduction, she generally
used a very appealing greeting or salutation. She was surprisingly inventive in
her charming and attractive manner of
saluting God and His elect. She delighted
to greet them through the sweet Heart of
Jesus, and that in an almost unlimited
variety of ways. Nearly every prayer of
St. Gertrude contains salutation, adoration,
praise, and thanksgiving, and at the end a
short, humble petition.

The predominant tone of all her prayers
is to offer the sacrificial life of Jesus Christ,
from His crib, where He weeps, bedded on
the straw, to that hour when on the Cross
He surrenders His Spirit into the hands of
His Father. The immeasurable love of the
Sacred Heart in the Holy Eucharist ravished Gertrude's soul. From this inexhaustible treasury, the holy virgin drew the
excellence, power and unction of her

prayers. Before the Sacrament of Love, her loving heart burst forth into songs of praise and joy, surpassing the understanding of men weighed down by earthly affections.

The charm, love, and affection with which the blessed Gertrude knew how to unite herself with our Savior, with His prayers, His sufferings, His Death, and merits, is beyond expression. Adorned with these treasures of infinite value, she was emboldened, we might say, and courageously entered, full of confidence, before the throne of the Triune God to render Him all honor and glory through Jesus Christ.

Oh, how touchingly and beautifully Gertrude knew how to describe to the Heavenly Father the sufferings, the cruel death and the infinite love of His only Son! When she prayed to the Most Holy Trinity, she offered, in a very ingenious manner, the perfections of each Divine Person. She praised the Father through the co-eternal Son, and the Son through the love and goodness of the Holy Spirit.

Who can express how tenderly and reverently the saint greeted and congratulated Mary, the Heavenly Queen! How intense and heartfelt was her compassion for the Dolorous Mother! She had an irresistible

way of inducing Mary to be most conde-
scending by saluting her through her Son,
and reminding her of the most tender affection which Jesus showed her during His
earthly life.

Marvelous to say, in nearly all her
prayers, Gertrude prayed, first, for a pure
and guileless heart, that no stain of sin
might defile her or mar the beauty of her
soul; and secondly, for a happy hour of
death. Even after she had been assured of
eternal glory, she did not desist from pray-
ing for this most important of all graces.
This is surprising to us, since this seraphic
virgin was as a spotless mirror. Her superhuman purity of heart was the admiration
of heaven. But she was destined to be a
guide to hundreds of thousands of souls,
and doubtless our Savior had in view the
needs of those persons who in subsequent
centuries would venerate and imitate her
and use her prayers to their great spiritual advantage.

Happy the soul who seeks to enter into
the spirit of Gertrude's prayers and to pray
as she did! Such a soul will easily rise above
self, above earthly inclinations and temporal cares. She, too, will love Our Lord and
His Blessed Mother. With joy and confi-

dence she, too, will approach the adorable Trinity, for from Gertrude she will have learned how to offer the most precious Gift to the Triune God—Jesus Christ with all His merits. She, too, will one day pray as did St. Gertrude, the mistress of prayer and seraph of Divine love.

Examples of
St. Gertrude's Prayers

Acts of Praise in Honor of the
Most Holy Trinity

I VENERATE and glorify Thee, O Most Blessed Trinity, in union with that ineffable glory with which God the Father, in His omnipotence, honors the Son and the Holy Spirit forever. **Gloria Patri**.

I magnify and bless Thee, O Most Blessed Trinity, in union with that most reverent glory with which God the Son, in His unsearchable wisdom, glorifies the Father and the Holy Spirit forever. **Gloria Patri**.

I adore and extol Thee, O Most Blessed Trinity in union with that most adequate and befitting glory with which the Holy Spirit, in His unsearchable goodness, extols the Father and the Son forever. **Gloria Patri**.

Offering of Our Savior's Life to the Eternal Father

O most loving Father, in atonement and satisfaction for all my sins I offer Thee the whole Passion of Thy most beloved Son, from the plaintive wail He uttered when laid upon the straw in the manger, through all the helplessness of His infancy, the privations of His boyhood, the adversities of His youth, the sufferings of His manhood, until that hour when He bowed His head upon the Cross and with a loud cry gave up His Spirit. And, in atonement and satisfaction for all my negligences, I offer Thee, O most loving Father, the most holy life and conversation of Thy Son, most perfect in His every thought, word, and action, from the hour when He came down from His lofty throne to the Virgin's womb, and thence came forth into our dreary wilderness, to the hour when He presented to Thy Fatherly regard the glory of His conquering flesh. Amen.

Devout Affections on the Passion of Our Lord Jesus Christ

It was revealed to St. Gertrude that reading and meditating on the Passion are far more useful and efficacious than all other spiritual exercises. As those who handle flour cannot avoid contracting some whiteness, so no one, however imperfect his devotion may be, can occupy his mind with the Passion of Our Lord without receiving some benefit therefrom. And, however cold and lukewarm our devotion, Our Lord will look upon us with greater long-suffering and mercy if we never omit the memory of His Passion.

First Prayer

O Lord Jesus Christ, the eternal sweetness and jubilee of those who love Thee, remember all the presentiment of grief Thou didst endure from the moment of Thy conception, and especially at Thy entrance into Thy Passion, when Thou didst say: **My soul is sorrowful even unto death**; and when, by reason of Thy overwhelming dread and anguish and grief, Thou didst sweat, as it were, drops of Blood trickling down upon the ground. Remember all the bitterness of Thy sorrow when Thou wast seized upon by the Jews, accused by false witnesses, condemned by Thy three judges, buffeted and smitten, spit upon, scourged, and crowned with thorns. O sweetest Jesus, I implore Thee, by all the sorrows and insults Thou didst endure, have mercy on me, a sinner. Amen.

Second Prayer

O Jesus, paradise of the delights of God, remember now all the dread and sorrow Thou didst endure when Pilate pronounced on Thee sentence of death; when the godless soldiers laid the heavy Cross on Thy shoulders, and fastened Thee thereon with rude and blunted nails, cruelly stretching Thy sacred limbs so that all Thy bones could be numbered: I beseech Thee, vouchsafe to pronounce a merciful sentence on me in the day of judgment, and deliver me from all punishment. Amen.

Third Prayer

O Jesus, Heavenly Physician, remember now the languor and the pain Thou didst endure when lifted upon the Cross, when all Thy bones were out of joint, so that no sorrow was like to Thy sorrow, because, from the sole of Thy foot to the top of Thy head, there was no soundness in Thee; when, notwithstanding, Thou didst put away the feeling of all Thine own griefs, and pray to Thy Father for Thine enemies, saying: **Father, forgive them; for they know not what they do**. By this, Thy charity and Thy mercy, grant that the dignity and worth of Thy Passion may be the entire remission of all my sins. Amen.

Fourth Prayer

O Jesus, mirror of the eternal splendor, remember now that sadness which filled Thy Heart when Thou didst behold in the mirror of Thy Divinity the reprobation of the wicked and the multitude of the lost; and by the depth of the compassion Thou didst show to the robber on the cross, saying: **This day thou shalt be with Me in paradise**, I beseech Thee, O compassionate Jesus, show me Thy mercy in the hour of my death. Amen.

Fifth Prayer

O Jesus, King most beloved, remember now the mournful desolation of Thy Heart, when Thou, forsaken by all, wert mocked as Thou didst hang on the Cross; when Thou didst find none to comfort Thee but Thy beloved Mother, who stood by Thy Cross to the last, and whom Thou didst commend to Thy disciple, saying: **Woman, behold thy son**, and to the disciple:

Behold thy Mother. I beseech Thee, O compassionate Jesus, by that sword of anguish which then pierced her Heart, do Thou condole with me and console me in all my tribulations. Amen.

Sixth Prayer

O Jesus, inexhaustible fountain of pity, remember now that bitterness which Thou didst endure when, Thy strength being exhausted and Thy sacred Body dried up, Thou didst feel that burning **thirst**, and hadst not one drop of water to cool Thy parched tongue, but only vinegar upon hyssop; I beseech Thee that Thou wouldst extinguish in me the thirst of carnal concupiscence and worldly delights. Amen.

Seventh Prayer

O Jesus, mighty King, remember now that when Thou wast plunged into the bitter waters of Thy Passion until they closed over Thy head, Thou wast forsaken not only by men but by Thy Father also, and didst cry out with a loud voice, saying: **My God, My God, why hast Thou forsaken Me?** By this Thine anguish and dereliction, I beseech Thee, forsake me not in my last agony. Amen.

Eighth Prayer

O Jesus, strong Lion of the tribe of Juda, remember now the sorrow and the woe Thou didst endure, when all the forces of Thy Heart and of Thy Flesh failed Thee utterly, and Thou didst bow Thy head and cry: **It is consummated**. By this Thine anguish and Thy woe, have mercy on me at the end of my life, when my soul shall be troubled, and my spirit disquieted within me. Amen.

Ninth Prayer

O Jesus, splendor of the Father's glory and figure of His substance, remember now that earnest commendation with which Thou didst commend Thy Spirit to the Father, saying: **Father, into Thy hands I commend My Spirit!** and when, Thy most sacred Body being torn and Thy Heart broken, and all the bowels of Thy compassion laid bare for our Redemption, Thou didst give up Thy Spirit: I beseech Thee, by all that love which moved Thee, the Life of all that live, to submit to death, that Thou wouldst mortify and kill in my soul whatever is displeasing to Thee. Amen.

Tenth Prayer

O Jesus, true and fruitful Vine, remember now the lavish, the excessive profusion wherewith Thou didst shed Thy Precious Blood, when on the Cross Thou didst tread the winepress alone, and wast crushed as a cluster of ripe grapes; when Thou didst give us water and Blood from Thy pierced Side, so that not one drop remained in Thy Heart. Then wast Thou hung up as a bundle of myrrh, and Thy tender Flesh grew pale, and Thy moisture was all dried up within Thee, and the marrow of Thy bones consumed. By this Thy most bitter Passion, and by the shedding of Thy most Precious Blood, I beseech Thee, O most loving Jesus, wash my soul at the hour of my death with the water which flowed from Thy Sacred Side, and adorn it with comeliness in the Precious Blood of Thy sweetest Heart, and render it acceptable in Thy sight in the fragrant odor of Thy Divine love. Amen.

Oblation

Accept, O compassionate Jesus, this my prayer with that exceeding love wherewith Thou didst endure a bitter Death, and didst offer it, together with all the fruit of Thy most sacred Humanity, to God the Father on the day of Thine ascension; and by the depth of those Wounds which scarred Thy flesh and pierced Thy hands and feet and Heart, I beseech Thee, raise me up, who am steeped and sunk in sin, and render me well-pleasing to Thee in all things. Amen.

A Most Tender and Efficacious Offering to the Blessed Virgin

O sweetest Jesus, I beseech Thee, by the love which caused Thee to take flesh in the bosom of this most pure Virgin, that Thou wouldst supply for our defects in the service and honor of this most benign Mother who is ever ready to assist us, with maternal tenderness, in all our necessities. Offer to Thy beloved Mother, O amiable Jesus, the superabundant beatitude of Thy sweetest Heart. Show her Thy Divine predilection which chose her from eternity, above all creatures, to be Thy Mother, adorning her with every grace and virtue. Remind her of all the tenderness which Thou didst manifest to her on earth, when she carried Thee on her bosom and nourished Thee with her milk. Recall to her Thy filial obedience to her in all things, and especially Thy care at the hour of Thy death, when Thou didst forget Thine own anguish to solace hers, and didst provide her with a faithful guardian. Remind her, also, of the joys and glory of her Assumption, when Thou didst exalt her above all the choirs of angels and constitute her Queen of heaven and earth. O good Jesus, make Thy Mother propitious to us, that she may be our advocate and protectress in life and in death. Amen.

Thanksgiving for Graces Bestowed on St. Gertrude

To implore favors through her merits

God revealed to St. Gertrude that those who should thank Him for the graces bestowed upon her would participate in her merits, and would obtain their petition provided it were for their eternal welfare.

O most sweet Lord Jesus Christ, I praise, extol and bless Thee, in union with that heavenly praise which the Divine Persons of the Most Holy Trinity mutually render to each other, and which thence flows down upon Thy sacred Humanity, upon the Blessed Virgin Mary and upon all the angels and saints. And I give Thee thanks for all the graces Thou didst lavish upon Thy beloved spouse, St. Gertrude. I thank Thee especially for that ineffable love wherewith Thou didst pre-elect her from all eternity, didst enrich her so highly, didst draw her so sweetly to Thyself by the strongest bonds of love, didst unite her so blissfully to Thyself, dwell with such delight in her heart, and crown her life with so blessed an end. I recall to Thee now, O most compassionate Jesus, the promise Thou didst make to Thy beloved spouse, that Thou wouldst most assuredly grant the prayers of all who come to Thee through her merits and intercession, in all matters concerning their salvation. I beseech Thee, by Thy most tender love, grant me the grace . . . which I confidently expect. Amen.

Prayer before Work

O Lord Jesus Christ, in union with Thy
most perfect actions I commend to Thee this
my work, to be directed according to Thy
adorable will, for the salvation of all
mankind. Amen.